THE HOME DISTILLING
& INFUSING HANDBOOK

SECOND EDITION

THE HOME DISTILLING & INFUSING HANDBOOK

MAKE YOUR OWN WHISKEY & BOURBON BLENDS, INFUSED SPIRITS, CORDIALS & LIQUEURS

MATT TEACHER

CIDER MILL PRESS

BOOK PUBLISHERS

Kennebunkport, Maine

13-Digit ISBN: 9781604335354
10-Digit ISBN: 1604335351

This book may be ordered by mail from the publisher. Please include $5.95 for postage and handling.
Please support your local bookseller first!

Books published by Cider Mill Press Book Publishers are available at special discounts for bulk purchases in the United States by corporations, institutions, and other organizations. For more information, please contact the publisher.

Cider Mill Press Book Publishers
"Where good books are ready for press"
12 Spring Street
PO Box 454
Kennebunkport, Maine 04046

Visit us on the Web! www.cidermillpress.com

Design by Alicia Freile, Tango Media

Photo Credits:
Shutterstock: pages 9, 11, 14, 18, 19, 20, 22, 24, 25, 26, 27, 28, 31, 39, 45, 62, 66, 67, 70, 89, 90, 99, 102, 107, 126, 134, 139, 146, 148, 154, 164, 176, 184, 188, 190, 192, 203, and 205.
Kitchen Konfidence: pages 36, 27, 48, 49, 50, 51, 52, 53, 55, 76, 78, 79, 80, 81, 82, 83, 86, 87, 95, 96, 97, 100, 101, 108, 109, 115, 116, 117, 118, 119, 122, 123, 124, 125, 128, 129, 130, 131, 136, 137, 144, 145, 150, 151, 152, 153, 158, 159, 160, 161, 166, 167, 168, 169, 178, 174, 175, 179, and 204.
Appleseed Press: pages 40, 41, 56, 57, 68, 69, 72, 73, 74 (middle ingredient shot), 75, 77, 84, 85, 91, 92, 93, 103, and 127.
Leslie Miller: pages 42, 43, 46, 47, 58, 59, 60, 64, 65, 74 (two ingredient shots), 104, and 105.
Courtesy of Khong River House: page 193.
Courtesy of The Eveleigh: page 197.

Printed in China

1 2 3 4 5 6 7 8 9 0
First Edition

CONTENTS

INTRODUCTION

A re you the kind of person who goes "off recipe" when cooking a big meal? Do you ever sit with a glass of bourbon mentally devising the different ways you can take this wonderful drink and make it even better? If you're a risk-taker who likes to dabble, invent, experiment, and concoct (especially when it comes to your alcoholic beverages), you've come to the right place! This book guides you step by step through the process of creating unique and delicious alcoholic infusions and blends as well as infused cordials and crèmes—all with simple ingredients and all within the confines of your home. You don't need a special degree or fancy equipment, just this book and a propensity for trying something new.

Take care to choose your ingredients wisely. The farm-to-table world we live in today is brimming with opportunities to pair fresh, local ingredients from farmers' markets and local outlets with spirits. Concurrently we enjoy the benefit of a global economy of trade, giving us the ability to source far-off fixings. With these two tools one can create some truly stunning concoctions. When purchasing fruits and vegetables for infusions, the closer to home it is grown, generally the better and fresher tasting. When seeking exotic ingredients the Internet can provide just about any herb or spice one can imagine. This handbook should be used for inspiration, but the sky truly is the limit when pairing your ingredients. Herein lies both a collection of somewhat simple recipes for the beginner as well as some more advanced infusions and cocktails from some of today's leading mixologists. Whatever flavors suit your palette, *The Home Distilling & Infusing Handbook* is here to get you started.

The craft of distillation holds within it both a winding history and a modern, pioneering spirit. For centuries the human race has found wonder and respite in a glass of hooch. From large mass-producers to the moonshine farmers and all the small-batch producers in between, today our planet yields a vast collection of alcoholic tinctures. The variety is bountiful thanks to our global trade routes—moving harvests of grain, fruit, spices, and botanicals—and the numerous crafting options available to the apt distiller. Credit must also be placed on the recent surge of small-batch distilleries opening their doors on a global scale.

This book is full of infusion recipes for the *home distiller:* a distiller limited in his or her licit options. Some claim infusion is a form a distillation, while others stand opposite. Nevertheless, the infusion process, for a master distiller, is but one tool resting on the tip of their bibulous paintbrush. For many spirits such as gin and flavored vodkas, macerating (or infusing) herbs, fruits, and other botanicals may play a key role in a label's creation. Some gin makers, for example, soak juniper berries or other botanicals in the base alcohol before succeeding rounds through the still take place. Even though you may not be able to build a still and go into business producing whiskey, it may be helpful to have a general understanding of common distilling methods and techniques. Understanding the thought that some producers put into creating the most pure neutral spirit leaves one with an appreciation for choosing an infusion base wisely—and an appreciation for using locally sourced farm-fresh ingredients when infusing at home.

THE LAW

❋ Laws governing home distilling are very strict and are markedly different state by state. Check your local and state laws.

❋ There are no laws against making infusions or home vatting, providing you use spirits purchased from retailers, wholesalers, or producers.

❋ You are not allowed to sell the blends and infusions you create. Homemade spirits and blends make terrific gifts and party favors, though.

❋ This book contains many resources and makes various recommendations, not all of which are legal in all areas of the United States and abroad. Please take it upon yourself to know the laws in your region.

ABC Crackdown in San Francisco

Recently, one of the hotbeds of infusions has been San Francisco. Some truly innovative creations were being offered at numerous bars in the area. The ABC, or the Alcoholic Beverage Commission, in California has ruled that bars making their own infusions are in fact breaking the law by altering liquor and selling it. Bars have been required to stop infusing. If you live in California, please contact your representative to put an end to this crackdown.

SAFETY

❈ When making cordials and crèmes, do not add sugar to any liquor with less than 18 percent alcohol. The yeast will eat up the sugar creating carbon dioxide. This creates carbonation and can cause the bottles to explode.

❈ Be aware of the containers you use for making your infusions. You do not want to use plastic bottles or jugs or old leaded crystal jars as they can transfer their chemical taste into your liquid. These containers can impart an unpleasant taste into your infusion and even dangerous chemicals (especially with the lead). Also, do not use any containers that have stored anything except other liquors or foods, as residue can corrupt the purity of the taste.

❈ Refrigerate any liqueurs or crèmes you make that contain dairy products.

DISTILLING

In its simplest from, as defined by Merriam-Webster, *distillation* is: *the process of purifying a liquid by successive evaporation and condensation.* Ancient alchemists discovered that by heating up a liquid made from fermented grains, fruits, or vegetables—all containing two key components: yeast and carbohydrates—they were able to separate the ethanol and then cool and collect it in a separate vessel. The key to distillation is that water evaporates at a temperature of 100 degrees Celsius while the ethanol turns to vapor first at 78.3 degrees. Control the heating element so that only the ethanol is boiling and we have the birth of the spirit!

Since then, technology and methodology have come a long way. The art of distillation has evolved into a process that employs countless variables and unending outcomes. From the water source of a vodka to the barrels used to age whiskeys, every variable counts.

Distilling is a science. It is a science with no exact cure and no unanimously procured perfection. Each distiller's methodology is unique as is each sipper's pallet. Each distiller must—in their own location and practice—create or purchase neutral source spirit, select added ingredients, select what still they will use, and choose their distillation methods.

Laws governing home distilling are very strict and are markedly different state by state. Please be sure to check your local and state laws before attempting any home distilling. However, there are no laws against making infusions or home vatting, provided you are using whiskeys purchased from retailers, wholesalers, or producers. Where distilling is legal, today's distiller has many options. Let's take a look at common practices used by some of the more successful spirit brands.

"MOST DISTILLERS choose not to rotate their barrels. Not us. We like ours to get out and move around. And by move around, we mean rotate. It ensures every barrel experiences the same aging process. And you know what they say: a moving barrel gathers no moss."

— MAKER'S MARK

BRANDY

Brandy is made from distilling fermented fruit, or wine. A distiller chooses their fruit base—common choices include peaches, apples, grapes, pears, and plums. The fruit is then cleaned, sectioned, and mashed in a glass or ceramic container. Dry active yeast is then added to the fruit to prompt the fermentation process. Sometimes, for less sweet fruit, sugar is added. Using in-season fresh fruits is key to a good brandy. The fermentation process takes about a month. The wine may then be bottled and aged to mature the flavor. Then at least two rounds of distillation are run to purify and refine the wine into a spirit. Often, especially with large-batch distilleries, the distillate is aged in oak casks.

"We all drew on the comfort which is given out by the major works of Mozart, which is as real and material as the warmth given up by a glass of brandy."

— REBECCA WEST

GIN

Gin is created with either neutral vodka or any other neutral spirit as its base. Distillers generally look for the smoothest, least flavorful base so that the chosen botanicals' essences are captured unadulterated. The only rule of classification for a gin is that the botanical line-up must include the juniper berry. In addition to juniper other popular choices are angelica root, coriander seeds, cardamom, saffron, and citrus fruits. There are several classifications of gin, but the most popular, the London dry style, generally boasts a juniper forward taste, with other botanicals in the background supporting and balancing the spirit. A distiller begins with their neutral spirit and must experiment with flavor combinations, ratios, and distillation time. Some distillers infuse or macerate some or all of the botanicals before the spirit is run through the still. When distilling, botanicals may be placed in mesh bags at the top of the still, which infuses the spirit as vapors rise and pass through. Distillers may also choose to place the botanicals directly into the spirit at the base of the still. After distillation the spirit is cut with water to bottling strength.

"The only time I ever enjoyed ironing
was the day I accidentally got gin
in the steam iron."

— PHYLLIS DILLER

VODKA

A good vodka is supposed to be smooth and neutral. It should be the transparent base for whatever other flavors the consumer fancies. Some distillers offer lines of flavored vodkas in addition to neutral labels. In recent years many new, creative, and sometimes wacky, flavors have come to market. To make a basic neutral vodka the distiller begins by fermenting either grain or vegetables. A distiller may also choose to use sugars, molasses, or fruits as the vodka's base, but these are less common. When using a base such as potato the addition of food-grade amylase enzyme powder is required. The first step is to heat the grain vegetal matter in water to break down the starches into sugars. Distiller's yeast is added and the mixture begins to ferment. After fermentation is complete the liquid, known as the "wash," is strained into a separate container. The wash is now ready to be run through a still. Many distillers run the spirit through the still multiple times, purifying and increasing alcoholic content with each pass. As an age-old craft, there are many variations distillers may choose to use, such as filtering the vodka through charcoal after distillation. Lastly the vodka must be blended with water to achieve bottling strength.

"Money, like vodka, turns a person
into an eccentric."

— Anton Chekhov

RUM

This widely popular beach-day favorite begins with sugarcane, which is crushed to extract the sugar juice. There are many variables and practices a distiller has to choose from when making a rum, differing widely between regions. The most common custom is to process the sugarcane juice into molasses—a byproduct of producing crystalline sugar. The molasses is then either exposed to yeast existing in the native environment or, if in a sterile setting, selected yeast cultures are added. Sometimes the cane juice itself will be heated and reduced to a syrup that is then fermented. Fermentation time can range from a couple hours to a couple weeks. Once the fermented juice has peaked, it is ready for distillation, which refines the liquid into a higher-alcohol, purer spirit. At this point the liquid is clear. Most types of rum are then aged in oak casks—sometimes in old whiskey and bourbon barrels—which darkens the spirit's hue and sophisticates its taste. Generally these casks are then blended together to ensure a consistent product and then cut with water to bottling strength.

"RUM, n. Generically, fiery liquors that produce madness in total abstainers."

— AMBROSE BIERCE

TEQUILA

Tequila is made from the Agave tequilana plant, generally referred to as *blue agave*, and is a chief product of Jalisco, Mexico. In fact, according to tequila's given status of Appellation of Origin, the title of "tequila 100% agave" is limited to production in five Mexican states: Michoacán, Guanajuato, Tamaulipas, Nayarit, and Jalisco. If the spirit is not created solely from blue agave (it must be at least 51% blue agave) and is not made within Mexico the spirit is simply called "tequila." After six to ten years, when an agave plant has reached maturation, its leaves are removed to reveal the heart, or piña, which is used to produce tequila. The hearts are then steam cooked—this converts complex carbohydrates into simple sugars ready for extraction. The piñas are crushed in order to separate the liquids from plant matter. Once strained the juice is ready for fermentation. Some producers add yeast to accelerate and control this fermentation process. After one to two weeks the fermented liquid is ready to be distilled. Most tequila is distilled at least two times before being aged in repurposed bourbon casks—most often made from American or French white oak—for varying degrees of time. Younger

tequilas, known as *Reposados*, may be aged for between two and twelve months, while an older variety, known as *Extra Añejos*, is aged for over three years. All "tequila 100% agave" must be labeled and sealed in Mexico, while "tequila" does not have that prerequisite.

WHISKEY, WHISKY, BOURBON, AND SCOTCH

While the term "whiskey" generally refers to the spirit produced in the United States and Ireland, "whisky" is often used to denote product produced in Great Britain and Canada. Scotch is made in Scotland where distillers are known for the practice of drying malted barley over peat fires, while bourbon is crafted in United States. Depending on region and laws, whiskey may be made from corn, rye, malted barley, wheat, or a combination of the aforementioned. Bourbon must be made with a recipe containing at least 51 percent corn. Scotch is generally made from malted barley. Regardless of base choice, the grains are steeped in hot water, turning the starches into sugar, prepping the "wort" for fermentation. Yeast is added to instigate fermentation. After fermenting, the solution is ready for distillation. A majority of whiskey is distilled in pot stills, but some distillers also employ column stills. After distillation all whiskey is aged. Across the globe there are

regulations on how long the spirit must rest in casks before blending and bottling. Scotch must be aged for a minimum of three years. Many whiskies are aged in burnt oak barrels, which have been "toasted" with a flame to bring out the oak's characteristics. Once desired maturation has been achieved, the whiskey may be blended with other casks and is cut with water and bottled.

Home Distilling

While infusing entices culinary creative types, distilling is a bigger commitment—even aside from legalities. Designing your own still is no small amount of engineering. Even if you buy a kit, you may have to do some soldering and sealing. Check out the instructional videos by Clawhammer Supply Co. (http://www.clawhammersupply.com/pages/moonshine-videos), and you'll probably opt to pick up spirits at the packy. But if you're a diehard, check your state laws and be sure you have a safety mask, glasses, and gloves as well as a torch, locking pliers, ball-peen hammer, a mace or dolly, and hosing for cooling water input and cooling water drainage. And then you'll need to discard any product that comes through before the liquid reaches 174 degrees, as it may contain methanol. Don't say we didn't warn you. Distilling is serious business.

Back during Prohibition, home-distilled spirits were called moonshine, and moonshine was typically made from corn. After all, corn farmers could make a lot more money on their crop if they mashed, fermented, and distilled it and sold it on the down low. For authentic moonshine, corn is the way to go for maximum authenticity and flavor. If you've gotten as far as building a copper still, you're probably not fazed by needing to use upwards of 10 pounds of grain. But many first-timers start by making "sugar shine" out of nothing more extraordinary than sugar, water, and the obligatory yeast. Or you can go halfsies and do a "thin mash" with some maize, some sugar.

Just like with infusing, distilling brings an element of experimentation. You can distill just about any combination of sugar, water, and yeast. Options for the sugar include grains, fruits, even honey. You'll find hundreds of options at www.moonshinerecipe.org.

And then just imagine infusing with your own moonshine!

Moonshine and Whiskies Defined

Bourbon Whiskey: An American spirit distilled from a minimum of 51 percent corn wash—most strongly linked to Kentucky distilleries. After distillation the whiskey must be aged for at least two years in new charred oak barrels.

Corn Whiskey: A corn whiskey must be made from a minimum of 80 percent corn mash.

Irish Whiskey: An Irish spirit that is required to be produced from yeast-fermented malted grain.

Moonshine: A spirit produced in secret to avoid taxation and legalities. There is no aging process after distillation.

Rye Whiskey: A whiskey made from rye grain—a minimum of 51 percent rye must be used in the United States—and aged for a minimum of two years in charred oak barrels.

Scotch Whisky: A Scottish spirit made with malted barley. Blended Scotch whisky may use other grains in addition to the barley. Often the spirit will be filtered with peat for an added smoky character. *Note: Single-malt Scotch whisky must be made exclusively from malted barley.*

Tennessee Whiskey: A similar spirit and process to bourbon but with the addition of the Lincoln County Process, which requires Tennesseans to filter the whiskey through sugar maple charcoal after distillation and before aging.

Wheat Whiskey: A spirit made from primarily wheat—a minimum of 51 percent in the United States.

For a full list of U.S. spirit classifications, visit http://www.ttb.gov/spirits" www.ttb.gov/spirits

INFUSIONS

What separates a mixologist from a bartender? The answer is: a lot more than you think. Bartenders are master mixers of existing drinks, while mixologists concoct *original* cocktails with precise ratios, blending flavors to excite the imbiber's pallet in unique and stimulating ways. Many professionals consider themselves mixologists when experimenting with ingredients and ratios to create a new cocktail and bartenders while serving drinks. So put your mixologist hat on and get ready to experiment.

The revival of handcrafted cocktails has given way to a boom in creativity. One of the most commanding tools a mixologist has is the power of infusion (also known as *maceration*). With it, you have the power to combine the essence of a habanero pepper into tequila, the know-how to extract the taste of a fresh orange into your vodka, and the inspiration to combine your whiskey with smoky bacon.

HIGH-ALCOHOL INFUSION RECIPES

The thing about *good* vodka or neutral grain spirit is that it doesn't have much flavor—just a smooth alcoholic texture that is usually obscured by whatever it's mixed with. It's the pallet awaiting your brush. Why not spice it up a bit and use this blank canvas to paint your chosen flavor profile? The fun doesn't stop once your infusion is complete; creating cocktails by pairing mixers and garnishes is the second half of the journey. It is good to keep in mind the type of cocktails you typically enjoy when choosing infusion ingredients. If you typically enjoy a Bloody Mary, why not try a spicy pepper infusion? If you love gin and tonics, perhaps a juniper and citrus infused vodka would suit your taste. Here are some classic combinations to get you started.

GRAPEFRUIT RUM

The grapefruit essence lends itself to warm summer nights, and it pairs with seafood as well as avocado and carrots. It's great for celebrating in Caribbean style or bringing the tropical sun into your winter-worn home.

25 oz. rum

1 large pink grapefruit

1. Slice the grapefruit and remove the peel.

2. Place sliced grapefruit in bottom of infusion jar.

3. Add rum and seal the jar.

4. Let infuse for 1–2 weeks out of direct sunlight, tasting and gently shaking regularly.

5. Strain the rum into a clean bottle and cap.

TIP

You may also include the zest from the grapefruit peel. Just be sure to only use the outer layer of the peel and not the white portion.

COCONUT RUM

Coconut rum is great for all things beach related. This is sure to spruce up a Piña Colada or a Hurricane. It pairs well with Thai and Caribbean food.

25 oz. white rum

1 coconut

1. Drill a hole in the coconut, and drain and discard the liquid.

2. Break up coconut into pieces and peel off shell.

3. Place coconut pieces in a food processor and shred.

4. Place shredded coconut in bottom of infusion jar.

5. Add rum and seal the jar.

6. Let infuse for 2 weeks out of direct sunlight, tasting and gently shaking regularly.

7. Strain the rum into a clean bottle and cap.

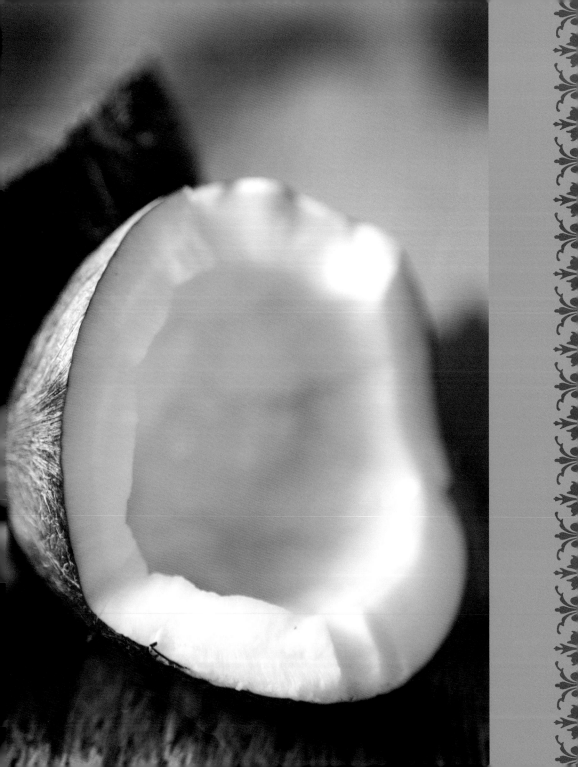

PEAR APPLE RUM

Having a party and need an exciting new cocktail to serve? Many great libations are at your fingertips with pear apple rum on hand. Try a spiced pear Appletini, which is sure impress guests' palates! All you need to do is mix infused rum, simple syrup (see page 113), fresh cinnamon, and lime juice for a beverage that perfectly captures the essence of early fall.

25 oz. rum

1 large red pear

4 red apples

1. Wash apples and pear.

2. Slice apples and pear into eighths.

3. Place sliced apples and pear in bottom of infusion jar.

4. Add rum and seal the jar.

5. Let infuse for 1–2 weeks out of direct sunlight, tasting and gently shaking regularly.

6. Strain the rum into a clean bottle and cap.

GINGER PINEAPPLE RUM

This infusion combines the sweetness of pineapple with the spice of ginger and is great beachside in a mojito or rum punch.

25 oz. rum

1 pincapplc

1 large piece of ginger

1. Slice the pineapple into cubes (rings work too).

2. Peel and cube the ginger.

3. Place pineapple and ginger in bottom of infusion jar. You may skewer the pineapple cubes instead of placing them freely in the jar if desired.

4. Add rum and seal the jar.

5. Let infuse for 1–2 weeks out of direct sunlight, tasting and gently stirring regularly.

6. Strain the rum into a clean bottle and cap.

TIP

For a less spicy outcome try adding the ginger a day or two after the pineapple.

LYCHEE RUM

The lychee is an exotic ingredient that has become increasingly popular in cocktails. This infusion is great for summertime sippers such as a daiquiri with a lychee for a garnish.

25 oz. rum

5 lychees

1. Cut around the stem of each lychee and twist it off.

2. Remove the seed from each lychee then squeeze the outside to pop the fruit out.

3. Place the lychee fruit in bottom of infusion jar and discard the peels.

4. Add rum and seal the jar.

5. Let infuse for 2–4 weeks out of direct sunlight, tasting and gently stirring regularly.

6. Strain the rum into a clean bottle and cap.

"Show me how you drink
and I will tell you who you are."

— EMILE PEYNAUD

BLACKBERRY CINNAMON RUM

The cinnamon really transforms rum from a summertime spirit into something to warm the soul on a winter's night.

25 oz. rum

4 cups fresh blackberries

2 cinnamon sticks

1. Wash the blackberries.

2. Place the blackberries and cinnamon sticks in bottom of infusion jar.

3. Add rum and seal the jar.

4. Let infuse for 1–2 weeks out of direct sunlight, tasting and gently stirring regularly.

5. Strain the rum into a clean bottle and cap.

TIP

Try a dash of this over vanilla ice cream!

CHERRY VODKA

Steeping cherries in vodka is a surefire way to add some sweetness and tartness to your vodka cocktails. Try it in a Cosmopolitan or Cherry Martini (with an alcoholic cherry as the garnish).

25 oz. vodka

8 cups cherries

1. Wash cherries.

2. Remove the stems and pit the cherries.

3. Place cherries in bottom of infusion jar.

4. Add vodka and seal the jar.

5. Let infuse for 5–7 days out of direct sunlight, tasting and gently shaking regularly until desired intensity is reached.

6. Strain the vodka into a clean bottle, cap, and refrigerate.

TIP

The vodka-soaked cherries make an excellent cocktail garnish.

JALAPEÑO PEPPER VODKA

Ready for some spice? This vodka is great for Sunday brunch Bloody Marys and a surefire cure for the weekend hangover.

25 oz. vodka

1–2 fresh jalapeño peppers

1. Wash jalapeño peppers.

2. Place whole peppers in bottom of infusion jar.

3. Add vodka and seal the jar.

4. Let infuse for 1–4 days out of direct sunlight, tasting and gently shaking regularly until desired intensity is reached.

5. Strain the vodka into a clean bottle, cap, and refrigerate.

TIP

If you want a more intense heat and spice, cut and deseed the peppers before infusing, The infusion time really depends on how spicy you want your vodka to be.

SUMMERTIME WATERMELON VODKA

Having a pool party this summer? Make some watermelon-infused vodka ahead of time and then create a refreshing poolside punch for your guests. The sweet character of this infusion is also a hit in vodka martinis and gimlets. Garnish with a fresh slice of watermelon for an aesthetic masterpiece.

25 oz. vodka

1 watermelon

1. Slice approximately one-sixth of a large watermelon into cubes. Do not include the rind.

2. Place cubed watermelon in bottom of infusion jar.

3. Add vodka, covering the watermelon cubes, and seal the jar.

4. Let infuse for 5–7 days out of direct sunlight, tasting and gently shaking regularly.

5. Strain the vodka into a clean bottle, cap, and refrigerate.

CUCUMBER VODKA

This subtle yet revitalizing infusion yields a cool, crisp libation. Make a batch of martinis, cosmos, or gimlets and pair with sushi or other fresh seafood.

25 oz. vodka

1½ cups cucumber

1. Wash, peel, and slice 1½ cups of cucumbers.

2. Place sliced cucumber in bottom of infusion jar.

3. Add vodka, covering the cucumber, and seal the jar.

4. Let infuse for 1–2 weeks out of direct sunlight, tasting and gently shaking regularly.

5. Strain the vodka into a clean bottle, cap, and refrigerate.

"Write drunk; edit sober."

— ERNEST HEMINGWAY

GRAPEFRUIT CLOVE VODKA

This infusion is a nice balance of summer sweetness and winter spice. Try this one in a Cosmopolitan or mixed with a 2:1 ratio of Coca-Cola to spirit.

25 oz. vodka

1 grapefruit

6 whole cloves

TIP

You may include some of the grapefruit rind, which contains a lot of flavorful oils, but make sure not to include the white pith.

1. Peel the grapefruit and separate into segments.

2. Place grapefruit and cloves in bottom of infusion jar.

3. Add vodka and seal the jar.

4. Let infuse for 1–2 weeks out of direct sunlight, tasting and gently stirring regularly.

5. Strain the vodka into a clean bottle and cap.

STRAWBERRY MINT VODKA

Bring the freshness of the garden to your glass. Try this one in a Vodka Martini or a Vodka Collins.

25 oz. vodka

5 cups chopped fresh strawberries

1 cup fresh mint leaves, bruised

1. Wash the strawberries and mint and discard the stems.

2. Half the strawberries.

3. Bruise the mint.

4. Place strawberries and mint in bottom of infusion jar.

5. Add vodka and seal the jar.

6. Let infuse for 1–3 weeks out of direct sunlight, tasting and gently stirring regularly.

7. Strain the spirit into a clean bottle and cap.

TIP

To bruise the mint leaves lightly tap the leaves with a pestle until they literally look a little bruised. Tapping too much will turn the mint bitter, so do it relatively quickly until approximately half the leaves look bruised.

APRICOT PEACH VODKA

Another summer favorite, this infusion really comes to life when crafted with locally sourced, fresh ingredients. Don't be afraid to experiment with the apricot-to-peach ratio to suit your pallet.

25 oz. vodka

4 fresh apricots

3 fresh peaches

1. Wash the apricots and peaches, half them, and remove and discard their pits.

2. Slice all fruit into quarters.

3. Place apricots and peaches in bottom of infusion jar.

4. Add vodka and seal the jar.

5. Let infuse for 1–2 weeks out of direct sunlight, tasting and gently stirring regularly.

6. Strain the spirit into a clean bottle and cap.

TIP

When picking out your apricots, look for a rich orange and reddish glow.

"I like to have a martini,
Two at the very most.
After three I'm under
the table, after four I'm
under my host."

— DOROTHY PARKER

BLOOD ORANGE CARDAMOM VODKA

This unique infusion will get your imagination going and will surely inspire custom cocktails in no time. Start by trying a blood orange vodka tonic!

25 oz. vodka

2 blood oranges

1½ cups whole cardamom

1. Peel the blood oranges and separate into segments.

2. Place blood oranges and cardamom in bottom of infusion jar.

3. Add vodka and seal the jar.

4. Let infuse for 1–2 weeks out of direct sunlight, tasting and gently stirring regularly.

5. Strain the spirit into a clean bottle and cap.

TIP

Try tasting the infusion's progress on the third day and every day after, waiting until you taste that perfect blend.

"THE MARTINI: the only American invention as perfect as the sonnet."

—H.L. MENCKEN

CARROT GINGER VODKA

This savory spicy infusion is enjoyable on a crisp fall day and makes an excellent Screwdriver, especially if made with freshly squeezed orange juice.

25 oz. vodka

3 large carrots

1 large piece of ginger

1. Peel the carrots and ginger and cut into sections.
2. Place carrots and ginger in bottom of infusion jar.
3. Add vodka and seal the jar.
4. Let infuse for 1–2 weeks out of direct sunlight, tasting and gently stirring regularly.
5. Strain the vodka into a clean bottle and cap.

TIP

For a less spicy outcome, try adding the ginger a couple days after the carrots.

LEMON VERBENA CANTALOUPE VODKA

This summer refresher compliments poolside living under a hot summer sun and makes for an excellent punch base. Make sure to use farm-fresh ingredients for this one—you're sure to notice the difference.

25 oz. vodka

¼ cup lemon verbena, bruised

½ cantaloupe

1. Rinse the lemon verbena, pluck from the stalk, and lightly bruise.

2. Cut the cantaloupe in half and then cube one half.

3. Place lemon verbena and cubed cantaloupe in bottom of infusion jar.

4. Add vodka and seal the jar.

5. Let infuse for 1–2 weeks out of direct sunlight, tasting and gently stirring regularly.

6. Strain the spirit into a clean bottle and cap.

TIP

To bruise the lemon verbena leaves lightly tap the leaves with a pestle until they literally looked a bit bruised— not too much!

GUMMY BEAR VODKA

Here's a fun one! This infusion is unique: depending on the time you allow your bears to infuse for you may be left with the bears only and very little liquid. As the bears absorb the vodka they swell turning into drunken gummy bears. Try serving these on a platter or as a cocktail garnish at your next party.

25 oz. vodka

2 cups gummy bears

1. Place gummy bears in bottom of infusion jar. You may also skewer them with space in between each bear and place them upright in the jar.

2. Add vodka and seal the jar.

3. Let infuse for at least 3 days out of direct sunlight, gently shaking regularly.

4. When the bears start to look plump remove one for tasting and continue daily until the desired amount of vodka has seeped in.

5. Strain what's left of the spirit into a clean bottle and cap. Store the bears in a sealed container.

TIP

Try finding gummy bears from your local candy shop as they tend to be softer and fresher.

CANDY CORN VODKA

This Halloween favorite might look appealing to youngsters, so make sure you set aside a secondary bowl of candy corn for *their* consumption. An example of the new fad of candy-infused alcohol, this vodka makes for a great dessert cocktail. Depending on infusion time, your infused vodka should have a bright, irresistible color and sweet taste to match.

25 oz. vodka

3 cups candy corn

1. Place candy corn in bottom of infusion jar.

2. Add vodka and seal the jar.

3. Let infuse for 2–5 days or more out of direct sunlight, tasting and gently shaking regularly.

4. Strain the vodka into a clean bottle, cap, and refrigerate.

TIP

Try using this infusion in a Candy Corn Martini.

There are lots of candies you can infuse with, such as jellybeans.

PUMPKIN VODKA

While the kids are out in search of candy, sit down with a few friends and enjoy a grown-up Halloween with a Pumpkin Martini. If your little ones (if you have little ones) are in need of a chaperone, this infusion will warm up your bones before a brisk fall evening walk.

25 oz. vodka

1 pumpkin (you won't use the whole thing)

1. Wash pumpkin.

2. Use a vegetable peeler to shave 12 thin ribbons (each approximately 6 inches in length) off the pumpkin.

3. Place pumpkin ribbons in bottom of infusion jar.

4. Add the vodka and seal the jar.

5. Let infuse for 1–2 weeks out of direct sunlight, tasting and gently shaking regularly until desired intensity is reached.

6. Strain the vodka into a clean bottle, cap, and refrigerate.

TIP

Add 5 or so cloves in the second week to step it up a notch.

ALMOND COFFEE VODKA

Although you may infuse the coffee grounds directly in the vodka and use several rounds through a French press to remove them, we recommend using pouches of grounds wrapped in cheesecloth and submerged in the vodka.

25 oz. vodka

1½ cups fresh almonds

1 cup fresh coffee beans

1. Grind the coffee beans and spoon the grinds into 3 or 4 small squares of cheesecloth. Make pouches by drawing the corners together, twisting, and then tying off with string.

2. Chop the almonds into small chunks.

3. Place coffee pouches and loose almonds in bottom of infusion jar.

4. Add vodka and seal the jar.

5. Let infuse for 1–2 weeks out of direct sunlight, tasting and gently stirring regularly.

6. Remove the pouches and strain the spirit into a clean bottle and cap.

TIP

You may experiment by adding simple syrup (page 113) to this recipe and turning it into a cordial.

HABANERO TOMATO VODKA

Wait for tomato season and try your hand at this warmer. It is recommended to skewer the tomato sections, leaving space in between each one, for best results. You may choose to skewer the peppers as well and can alternate between tomato and pepper for supreme flavor dispersion.

25 oz. vodka

2 fresh tomatoes

2 fresh habanero peppers

1. Wash the tomatoes and peppers.

2. Slice pepper tops off, and cut in half lengthwise.

3. Remove all seeds, but leave the ribbing.

4. Slice the tomatoes into quarters and skewer.

5. Place tomato skewers and peppers in infusion jar.

6. Add vodka and seal the jar.

7. Let infuse for 3–14 days out of direct sunlight, tasting and gently stirring regularly.

8. Remove the skewers and strain the spirit into a clean bottle and cap.

TIP

Try this one in a spicy Bloody Mary.

VANILLA VODKA

Want to be prepared to impress those unexpected guests? Vanilla Vodka is a great all-purpose infusion to have kicking around. Use it for White or Black Russians, Martinis, or a Screwdriver.

25 oz. vodka

2 whole vanilla beans

1. Wash vanilla beans.

2. Slice both beans open but not in half.

3. Place vanilla beans in bottom of infusion jar.

4. Add vodka, covering the beans, and seal the jar.

5. Let infuse for 1–2 weeks out of direct sunlight, tasting and gently shaking regularly.

6. Strain the vodka into a clean bottle, cap, and refrigerate.

RASPBERRY VODKA

Raspberry Vodka's fresh redolent quality complements a variety of cocktails. Try serving Raspberry Vodka Martinis at Sunday brunch. You may be surprised how good a Raspberry Bloody Mary can be. Sounds a little off, but don't judge until you've tried.

25 oz. vodka

⅔ cup raspberries

1. Wash raspberries.
2. Place raspberries in bottom of infusion jar.
3. Add vodka, covering the raspberries, and seal the jar.
4. Let infuse for 1–2 weeks out of direct sunlight, tasting and gently shaking regularly.
5. Strain the vodka into a clean bottle, cap, and refrigerate.

EARL GREY GIN

A mild Earl Grey infusion can be well suited for many cocktails. The Earl Grey will impart a refreshing earthy tone that complements the gin's juniper and coriander zest. Impress your friends with your custom Earl Grey Gin and Tonic with a sprig of fresh mint at a spring gathering.

1 liter (34 oz.) gin

¼ cup of loose Earl Grey tea leaves

1. Place loose tea leaves in bottom of infusion jar.

2. Add gin, covering the tea leaves, and seal the jar.

3. Let infuse for approximately 2 hours out of direct sunlight.

4. Strain the gin into a clean bottle, cap, and refrigerate.

TIP

Tea infuses quickly, so keep an eye on it.

RASPBERRY GIN

This summertime infusion goes great with an outdoor picnic or for sitting by the pool. Whip up a Negroni, a Gin Fizz, or your favorite summertime cocktail, and step into the sun!

25 oz. gin

⅔ cup raspberries

1. Wash raspberries.

2. Place raspberries in bottom of infusion jar.

3. Add gin, covering the raspberries, and seal the jar.

4. Let infuse for 1–2 weeks out of direct sunlight, tasting and gently shaking regularly.

5. Strain the gin into a clean bottle, cap, and refrigerate.

CUCUMBER GIN

This cucumber-infused gin is great in a Martini, a Gibson, or the lesser-known Gin Rickey (typically made with bourbon). Or drink this infusion as-is alongside a seafood dinner.

25 oz. gin

1½ cups cucumber

1. Wash, peel, and slice 1½ cups of cucumbers.
2. Place sliced cucumber in bottom of infusion jar.
3. Add gin, covering the cucumber, and seal the jar.
4. Let infuse for 1-2 weeks out of direct sunlight, tasting and gently shaking regularly.
5. Strain the gin into a clean bottle, cap, and refrigerate.

TIP

Use fresh cucumber slices as a garnish.

BOTANICAL BLENDS FOR INFUSED GIN

Here are a couple botanical combinations to get you started crafting a flavor profile for an infused, or *cold-compound*, gin at home. Whenever possible, procure fresh ingredients. Use either a neutral vodka or grain spirit as your base.

CITRUS LOVERS' INFUSED GIN

25 oz. grain spirit
or vodka

¼ cup juniper berries

⅛ cup coriander seeds

1 fresh lemon (peel)

1 fresh orange (peel)

1. Using a paring knife or vegetable peeler, peel the lemon and orange, making as many 1-inch-wide strips from the peel as possible.

2. Place all ingredients in the bottom of the infusion jar.

3. Add spirit and seal the jar.

4. Let infuse for 3–14 days out of direct sunlight, tasting and gently stirring regularly.

5. Strain the spirit into a clean bottle and cap it.

TIP

When peeling the citrus fruits make sure to use only the outer layer of the peel and not the white pith portion, which is very bitter.

LICORICE LOVERS' INFUSED GIN

25 oz. grain spirit
or vodka

¼ cup juniper berries

⅛ cup cardamom seeds

½ cup star anise

⅛ cup fennel seeds

1 fresh lemon (peel)

1. Using a paring knife or vegetable peeler, peel the lemon, making as many 1-inch-wide strips from the peel as possible.

2. Place all ingredients in the bottom of the infusion jar.

3. Add spirit and seal the jar.

4. Let infuse for 3–14 days out of direct sunlight, tasting and gently stirring regularly.

5. Strain the spirit into a clean bottle and cap it.

TIP

You may use chopped fennel leaves in addition to seeds in this infusion if desired.

YELLOW BEET GIN

These days, gins from around the world are being crafted with a vast array of herbs, spices, fruits, and vegetables, but, as far as we know, no one is using the beet!

25 oz. London dry gin

2 fresh beets

1. Wash beets.

2. Slice beets.

3. Place beets in bottom of infusion jar. You may also choose to skewer the slices and stand them up in the jar.

4. Add gin and seal the jar.

5. Let infuse for 3–14 days out of direct sunlight, tasting and gently stirring regularly.

6. Strain the gin into a clean bottle and cap.

TIP

Try to find fresh beets that are firm with a deep golden hue.

TOASTED SESAME SEED GIN

Adding the essence of sesame seeds to a spirit can make for some interesting cocktails. Try a Toasted Sesame Seed Martini alongside sushi.

25 oz. London dry gin

1½ cups sesame seeds

1. Toast sesame seeds in a pan over low heat until they begin to darken.

2. Place sesame seeds in bottom of infusion jar.

3. Add gin and seal the jar.

4. Let infuse for 2–4 weeks out of direct sunlight, tasting and gently stirring regularly.

5. Strain the gin into a clean bottle and cap.

TIP

Use a classic London dry gin such as Beefeater as the base.

{ WHISKEY }
SMOKED BACON BOURBON

This infusion is good for sipping by the fire after a big dinner. If drinking neat or with whiskey stones, add one or two drops of water before sipping. This will open up the bourbon's aromatic nature. It's also flavorsome chilled with an ice cube or two.

25 oz. bourbon

3-4 strips of smoky bacon (30 ml bacon fat)

1. Fully cook 4 strips of bacon in a pan.

2. Remove the bacon from the pan (eat or discard).

3. Let the bacon fat cool but not solidify.

4. Measure out 30 ml of rendered bacon fat.

5. Pour bacon fat into infusion jar.

6. Add bourbon and seal the jar.

7. Let infuse for between 1–2 days or more, out of direct sunlight, gently shaking regularly.

8. After desired taste is achieved, place in freezer overnight. This will cause the fat to congeal and separate from the alcohol, making it easy to strain.

9. Strain the whiskey into a clean bottle and cap.

TIP

Use smoky bacon to really get the flavor and aroma infused into your whiskey. You may also include the actual strips of bacon in the infusion.

BLUEBERRY BOURBON

Blueberries and bourbon … who would have thought? This infusion makes a surprisingly good Manhattan or Mint Julep on a warm summer's eve. Many find it appealing over ice cream as well.

1 liter (34 oz.) bourbon

1 cup blueberries

1. Wash blueberries.
2. Place blueberries in bottom of infusion jar.
3. Slightly muddle blueberries—break them slightly open, but leave them whole.
4. Add bourbon and seal the jar.
5. Let infuse for 2–5 days out of direct sunlight, tasting and gently shaking daily.
6. Strain the bourbon into a clean bottle and cap.

CHERRY WHISKEY

The cherry essence imparts sweet and tart components to a quality whiskey. The degree is dependant upon the type of cherries used and infusion time. It makes beautiful Manhattans and the infused cherries not only look great as a garnish, but also pack a punch. Might be wise to limit one cherry per person (or at least one per drink).

25 oz. whiskey

8 cups cherries

1. Wash, stem, and pit the cherries.

2. Place cherries in bottom of infusion jar.

3. Add whiskey, covering the cherries, and seal the jar.

4. Let infuse for 2–7 days out of direct sunlight, tasting and gently shaking regularly until desired intensity is reached.

5. Strain the whiskey into a clean bottle, cap, and refrigerate.

Adding Water to Cocktails

Adding a little spring water to your whiskey can actually enhance the aroma while cutting some of the burn. Aroma molecules evaporate a good deal better in water than alcohol. This is because aroma molecules are closer chemically to alcohol. Add a little water and take a smell. This applies to anything with high alcohol content, including wines.

HABANERO PEPPER TEQUILA

After your infusion has reached the desired spice intensity, rack or strain the liquor and concoct some spicy margaritas. For the extremely brave, a fresh habanero ring may be used as a garnish.

25 oz. tequila

3 habanero peppers

1. Wash habanero peppers.

2. Slice pepper tops off, and cut in half lengthwise.

3. Remove all seeds, but leave the ribbing.

4. Place the halved peppers in bottom of infusion jar.

5. Add tequila and seal the jar.

6. Let infuse for 3 days or more in a cool place out of direct sunlight, tasting and gently shaking regularly until desired intensity is reached.

7. Strain the tequila into a clean bottle and cap.

TIP

Do not leave the pepper seeds in. They will overpower the whole infusion. If you'd like more spice, add another seeded pepper.

PINEAPPLE TEQUILA

Can you feel the warm sun on your face as you imbibe the first taste of your new pineapple tequila infusion? This was made for frozen margaritas on a warm sunny day. Pair with fresh seafood such as shrimp or scallops.

25 oz. tequila

1 pineapple

1. Slice the pineapple into chunks (rings work too).
2. Place pineapple chunks in bottom of infusion jar.
3. Add tequila, covering the pineapple, and seal the jar.
4. Let infuse for 1–2 weeks out of direct sunlight, tasting and gently shaking regularly.
5. Strain the tequila into a clean bottle, cap, and refrigerate.

LEMONGRASS CUCUMBER TEQUILA

This one makes for a great summer margarita. Try adding a slice of fresh cucumber garnishment for that extra zing.

25 oz. tequila

1 fresh cucumber

1 cup chopped lemongrass

1. Wash the lemongrass and cucumber.

2. Peel the cumber and slice.

3. Chop the lemongrass into approximately 1-inch sections.

4. Place lemongrass and cucumber in bottom of infusion jar.

5. Add tequila and seal the jar.

6. Let infuse for 2–4 weeks out of direct sunlight, tasting and gently stirring regularly.

7. Strain the tequila into a clean bottle and cap.

TIP

You may choose to skewer the cucumber slices and stand them up in the jar.

HONEYSUCKLE TEQUILA

The best way to go about making this infusion is to wait until honeysuckle season and go out and procure your own. Try this summer sweetener in a Tequila Sunrise cocktail.

25 oz. tequila

2 cups honeysuckle

1. Remove the green part from each honeysuckle.
2. Place honeysuckles in bottom of infusion jar.
3. Add tequila and seal the jar.
4. Let infuse for 2–4 weeks out of direct sunlight, tasting and gently stirring regularly.
5. Strain the tequila into a clean bottle and cap.

"One tequila, two tequila, three tequila, floor."

—GEORGE CARLIN

WALNUT COGNAC

Walnut Cognac is the glass you want by your side on a cold winter's night. Try sipping this neat (no ice) out of a snifter. The toasty nutty flavor complements a sweet desert or a nice cigar.

25 oz. cognac

2 cups shelled walnuts

1. Shell walnuts.

2. Toast walnuts in the oven for 15 minutes at 400°F on a baking sheet.

3. Place walnuts in bottom of infusion jar.

4. Add cognac and seal the jar.

5. Let infuse for 5–7 days out of direct sunlight, tasting and gently shaking regularly.

6. Strain the cognac into a clean bottle and cap.

LOW-ALCOHOL INFUSION RECIPES

Cordials and crèmes are infusions that generally contain a smaller amount of alcohol (17–30 percent) and are sweeter, due to the addition of simple syrup or other sweeteners. When making liqueurs, many find it is best to use as neutral a palette as possible. Although not available in all states, the best choice for a neutral alcoholic base is high-proof grain alcohol.

If pure grain alcohol is not available in your state, the next best choice is non-flavored vodka. In the United States, all non-flavored vodka is legally required to be odorless, colorless, and tasteless, but that's not to say equal. Choose a quality vodka wisely. If you're interested in showcasing the fresh purity of your ingredients, this is the best choice. Although not as widely used, other choices for your alcoholic base are brandy, rum, whiskey, and gin.

After you have chosen your alcoholic base, choose your fruits, nuts, herbs, spices, or flavored extracts.

Although most cordials and crèmes are made with simple syrup (made from sucrose or table sugar), there are other options to consider based on your desired outcome. Some other options include: honey, brown sugar, or corn syrup, all of which have a distinctive flavor. As with any ingredient substitute, know that it will affect the taste of your end result.

Racking vs. Straining

For cordials and crèmes you may prefer to use the racking method to filter out the fruits, nuts, herbs, and spices. Filtering through coffee filters or cheesecloth can take a long time with thicker liquors.

What You Need

- Approximately 3 feet of clear plastic tubing (you can find it at any pet supply store sold for aquariums)
- Matured infusion in original jar
- An additional infusion jar or suitable container

What You Do

1. Place the jar containing the matured infusion on an elevated surface.
2. Place the second clean jar on a surface that is lower than the first jar. (The kitchen sink or bathtub works well).
3. Feed one end of the plastic tubing into the jar containing the liqueur until it's 1 or 2 inches from the settled ingredients at the bottom. (Do not disturb the sediment at the bottom of the jar.)
4. Suck on the other end of the tube, like a straw, to get the liquid flowing, and then place it in the second lower jar.
5. The liquid will flow through the tube into the clean jar, leaving the solids in the original jar.

How to Make Simple Syrup

1. Combine equal parts sugar and water in a saucepan.

2. Bring to a boil over medium-high heat.

3. Stir continuously until all the sugar has dissolved and the liquid is clear. Make sure not to burn the sugar.

4. Remove from heat and store in a container for future use.

Note: Experiment with the ratio of water to sugar. For some infusions, thicker simple syrup may be more desirable.

"Candy is dandy but liquor is quicker."

— OGDEN NASH

PINEAPPLE BASIL CORDIAL

This refreshing cordial complements any lazy summer day by the pool. It's also fantastic for entertaining friends and family for brunch. Pair with a light fare menu of quiche, fresh fruit, and finger sandwiches. This cordial combines the tropical fruit with the fresh herbs of a summertime garden.

25 oz. grain alcohol or non-flavored vodka

1 pineapple

3 tablespoons fresh chopped basil

1. Slice the pineapple into rings.

2. Chop basil.

3. Combine pineapple and basil in bottom of infusion jar.

4. Pour in alcohol, covering pineapple and basil, and seal the jar tightly.

5. Let infuse for 30 days or more in a cool place out of direct sunlight, tasting and remixing daily until desired intensity is reached.

6. Strain or rack the cordial into a clean bottle.

7. Add simple syrup (page 113) to taste and tightly cap.

8. Let it rest out of direct sunlight for at least 30 days, preferably a year or more.

TIP

You can also add a splash of pineapple juice to this infusion.

STRAWBERRY ROSEMARY CORDIAL

Summer in a bottle! Let the sun sparkle off the beautiful red and pink hues of this sweet berry-and-garden inspired beverage. Share a glass or two with a loved one on the front porch or deck: garnish with fresh berries or a sprig of mint.

25 oz. white brandy

5 cups chopped fresh strawberries

5 sprigs fresh rosemary

1. Wash, stem, and halve strawberries.

2. Place strawberries in bottom of infusion jar.

3. Pour in brandy, covering the strawberries.

4. Place rosemary into alcohol, submerging the strawberries, and seal the jar tightly.

5. Let infuse for 1–3 months or more in a cool place out of direct sunlight, tasting and remixing daily until desired intensity is reached.

6. Strain or rack the cordial into a clean bottle.

7. Add simple syrup (page 113) to taste and tightly cap.

8. Let it rest out of direct sunlight for at least 30 days, preferably a year or more.

OCTOBER APPLE LIQUEUR

As the leaves are exploding with color and the air turns crisp and cold, warm up your friends and family with the quintessential essence of fall: fresh apples. Have a glass after raking the leaves or drizzle over pound cake for an autumn-inspired dessert.

17 oz. grain alcohol or non-flavored vodka

8½ oz. brandy

2½ pounds fresh apples

3 cinnamon sticks

1. Wash, stem, and slice apples in eighths.

2. Place apples and cinnamon sticks in bottom of infusion jar.

3. Pour in grain alcohol or vodka and brandy, covering the apples and cinnamon sticks, and seal the jar tightly.

4. Let infuse for 1–2 months in a cool place out of direct sunlight, tasting and gently shaking daily until desired intensity is reached.

5. Strain or rack the cordial into a clean bottle.

6. Add simple syrup (page 113) to taste and cap tightly.

7. Let it rest out of direct sunlight for at least 30 days, preferably a year or more.

TIP

After straining your apples from the liqueur, place apples in a large re-sealable bag and crush to release the absorbed alcohol. Then filter out small apple pieces through a fine cheesecloth and pour liquid back into the liqueur with the simple syrup.

"There can't be good living where there is not good drinking."

— BENJAMIN FRANKLIN

PISTACHIO LIQUEUR

Celebrating life with a family-style Italian feast? Serve this nutty liqueur after dinner to complement a dark chocolate dessert. Sip slowly and enjoy this smooth and rich digestif.

17 oz. grain alcohol or non-flavored vodka

1 teaspoon pistachio extract flavoring

1 teaspoon glycerin

Food coloring (optional)

8½ oz. simple syrup (page 113)

1. Combine grain alcohol or vodka, and pistachio extract in an infusion jar.

2. Add glycerin and food coloring to simple syrup.

3. Pour simple syrup mix into infusion jar, stir and cap tightly.

4. Let it infuse for 1–2 months in a cool place out of direct sunlight, tasting and gently shaking regularly until desired intensity is reached.

TIP

Adding glycerin to your cordial will thicken it.

PRUNE LIQUEUR

Get the party moving with this fruit-infused spirit! Sip this delicious beverage, use it for cooking, or pair with a ricotta cheesecake for a spectacular dessert.

17 oz. grain alcohol or non-flavored vodka

8½ oz. brandy

1 pound dried pitted prunes

TIP

Many infusionists add food coloring to achieve a desired color.

1. Chop prunes into quarters.

2. Place prunes in bottom of infusion jar.

3. Pour in grain alcohol or vodka and brandy, covering the prunes, and seal the jar tightly.

4. Let infuse for 2–3 months in a cool place out of direct sunlight, tasting and gently shaking daily until desired intensity is reached.

5. Strain or rack the liquid into a clean bottle.

6. Add simple syrup (page 113) to taste and cap tightly.

7. Let it rest out of direct sunlight for at least 30 days, preferably a year or more.

BLACKBERRY HONEY BRANDY CORDIAL

Relax fireside with a glass and share a slow dance with your partner. Don't be afraid to drizzle this cordial over some homemade vanilla ice cream!

25 oz. brandy

4 cups fresh blackberries

Honey or simple syrup (page 113)

1. Wash blackberries.

2. Place blackberries in bottom of infusion jar and muddle slightly by pressing on them so they open but do not split completely in half.

3. Pour in brandy, covering the blackberries, and seal the jar tightly.

4. Let infuse for 1 week in a cool place out of direct sunlight, tasting and gently shaking daily until desired intensity is reached.

5. Strain or rack the liquid into a clean bottle.

6. Add honey or simple syrup to taste, stir, and cap tightly.

7. Let it steep for one week or longer.

PLUM LIQUEUR

Serve this liqueur alone, on the rocks, or bottle it up as a lovely holiday gift. Pairs well with dark chocolate, black tea, grapes, and raspberries for an after-dinner treat.

17 oz. grain alcohol or non-flavored vodka

8½ oz. brandy

3 pounds Damson plums

Sugar, to coat plums

Simple syrup (page 113)

TIP

You may add 1 cup of water if needed while mixing the sliced plums and sugar.

1. Wash, stem, and slice plums in eighths.

2. In a mixing bowl, combine plums and sugar and mix until sugar is dissolved.

3. Place plums in bottom of infusion jar.

4. Pour in grain alcohol or vodka and brandy, covering the plums, and seal the jar tightly.

5. Let infuse for 3 months in a cool place out of direct sunlight, tasting and gently shaking daily until desired intensity is reached.

6. Strain or rack the liquid into a clean bottle.

7. After straining plums from the liqueur, place plums in a large re-sealable bag and crush to release the absorbed liquid. Then filter out small plum pieces through a cheesecloth and pour liquid back into the liqueur.

8. Add simple syrup to taste, stir, and cap tightly.

9. Let it rest out of direct sunlight for at least 30 days.

LAVENDER LIQUEUR

Dreaming of simpler, more relaxed times? Let this lavender-infused liqueur bring you back to peaceful, simpler days. Garnish with mint, serve ice cold, or add sweet rose petals or honey for the perfect afternoon luncheon.

25 oz. grain alcohol or non-flavored vodka

6 tablespoons dried lavender pedals

1 cup simple syrup (page 113)

1. Place dried lavender pedals in bottom of infusion jar.

2. Pour in grain alcohol or vodka, covering the pedals, and seal the jar tightly.

3. Let infuse for 1 week or more in a cool place, tasting and gently shaking daily until desired intensity is reached.

4. Strain or rack the liquid into a clean bottle.

5. Add simple syrup, stir, and cap tightly.

6. Let it rest out of direct sunlight for an additional week or two.

KAHLÚA CRÈME

Spruce up your coffee with Kahlúa Crème. This crème is also delicious served over ice or drizzled atop ice cream. This is a favorite to bottle up for spectacular holiday gifts. Who doesn't love the taste of homemade Kahlúa?

25 oz. grain alcohol or non-flavored vodka

16–18 cups water

6 teaspoons strong dry instant coffee

2 pounds light brown sugar

5 teaspoons vanilla extract

1. Combine water and coffee in a large pot on the stove and bring to a boil.

2. Reduce heat to low.

3. Gradually add brown sugar and bring back to a boil while stirring continuously.

4. Turn off heat and allow to cool completely. Throw in a few ice cubes to speed this process up.

5. Add vanilla extract and grain alcohol or vodka and mix well.

6. Funnel into clean bottle and cap tightly. You may serve right away, but the taste does mature well.

TIP

You may use dark brown sugar for a richer molasses taste.

BOURBON & WHISKEY BLENDS

The making of home whiskey and bourbon blends (home vatting) is the process of taking two or more store-bought, single-malt whiskies and blending them together to create a custom flavor suited to your palette. Experimenting with the blending process will allow you to really get a sense of each whiskey's characteristics and how they interact. Don't ever dispose of a whiskey that you feel is not suited to your palette. These may still add a positive characteristic to a blend, and you won't end up wasting a bottle.

For the first time, start by choosing two whiskies that have unique and different characteristics. In subsequent blends, don't be afraid to try combining as many different whiskies as your taste buds desire. You may not always like the result, but no risk, no reward.

Initially choose one primary whiskey whose flavor you enjoy and add a smaller percentage of a whiskey that has a distinct characteristic. Maybe you have a lower end whiskey that is too smoky or spicy for your taste but might add complexity when blended with another single malt you enjoy. Adding a smaller portion of that to a whiskey lacking that characteristic can produce desired results. Start with a conservative portion of the lesser whiskey. You can always add more later.

Don't forget to log your blends. Keep a notebook with the whiskeys, ratios, and maturations times you've tried. Log each single malts alcohol content and calculate your finished blends alcohol by volume content as well. This will help you to refine your blends and figure out what you most enjoy.

American Whiskey

American whiskey is divided into six main categories: Bourbon, Tennessee, Rye, Corn, Wheat, and Blends. See the glossary for each alcohol's detailed attributes.

"The water was not fit to drink. To make it palatable, we had to add whisky. By diligent effort, I learned to like it."

— WINSTON CHURCHILL

MAKING A WHISKEY BLEND

After you've chosen two or more single malts, gather these items and you'll be ready to start.

1 bottle each of two or more brands of single-malt whiskey

2 glass decanters (at least 25 oz.) with tight-fitting stoppers (you may also use clean whiskey bottles)

Measuring cup

Calculator

1. Log single malt names, alcohol by volume content, and chosen ratios.

2. Measure desired proportions of each whiskey and combine in clean glass jar.

3. Seal jar and store out of direct sunlight for maturation, tasting regularly. The vatting process can last anywhere from a few days to years.

4. Transfer the matured blend into the clean jar and seal tightly. The blend is ready to be served.

TIP

You may use an oak barrel instead of glass jars to mature your blends. This gives the vatter another tool to instill flavor. Many professional distilleries rotate their barrels throughout the vatting process to keep the blends consistent and mixed well.

Barrel Toasting

The meticulous process of building a barrel from scratch is only the first stage in its long-lasting creation. After assembly, barrels are generally toasted to bring out the characteristics of the wood (conventionally variants of oak). The amount of time a barrel is exposed to flame—barrels may be toasted from *light* to *heavy*—change the wood's character as tannins are subdued and withheld flavors pronounced.

Infusing in Tight Quarters

Not many home infusers and blenders have a vast amount of space to dedicate solely to the craft, and most don't need to produce large batches. Fortunately, many online retailers and specialist distilling outlets offer smaller barrels for your convenience.

Blending and Aging

Many factors go into making your perfect whiskey blend: choice of complimentary yet diverse whiskies, whiskey ratios, barrel make and type, barrel toasting level, storage environment, and time at rest.

Whiskey Blends vs. Single-Malt

Single-malt whiskey is a spirit made from the blending of barrels from a single distillery. It does not mean that the spirit is comprised of only one barrel's contents—those are labeled *single-barrel*. Blended whiskey is made by combining batches together from two or more distilleries.

FEATURED INFUSIONS

Today many venues pride themselves on crafting homemade spirit infusions, syrups, and tonics for use in their cocktails, making a customer's experience truly unique. *The Home Distiller's Handbook* is filled with a diverse catalog of infusions to get the beginner up and running, but in order to satisfy the more adventurous I sought out some of today's leading mixologists to bring bar-quality infusions to your home arsenal. This chapter takes a look at what some of the cutting-edge craftsmen are infusing in-house and serving up in venues across the United States. They have graciously shared recipes for their favorite infusions and the cocktails they serve them in. Here is a selection of some of the best from celebrated mixologists across the nation!

THE OYSTER HOUSE
(KATIE LOEB)

The Oyster House is located in Center City, Philadelphia. Owned by the third generation of the Mink family to operate a raw bar in Philadelphia, Oyster House has taken infusions to a whole new level. Head bartender and Mixologist Katie Loeb crafts delectable infusions and serves them in the form of oyster shooters. This, along with house-made Aquavit, complements the raw bar and provides a savory means of combining oysters with a cocktail at the same time.

The following drinks are by Katie Loeb, former head mixologist/ bartender, Oyster House, Philadelphia, Pennsylvania.

AQUAVIT

This can be served ice cold in small-stemmed cordial glasses, in a Bloody Viking with your favorite Bloody Mary mix, or used as a cocktail ingredient.

2 liters good quality vodka (Katie uses Laird's for this drink)

3 tablespoons caraway seed

2 tablespoons dill seed

2 tablespoons cumin seed

1 tablespoon coriander seed

1 tablespoon fennel seed

2 star anise

3 whole cloves

4 strips each, orange and lemon peel (no pith)

1 ounce demerara sugar syrup, separated

1. Preheat oven to 400°F.

2. Place seeds on a foil-lined cookie sheet or sizzle plate. Toast lightly in the oven for 6-8 minutes, stirring every few minutes until warm and fragrant.

3. Remove and cool slightly. Crush seeds lightly and place into large airtight infusion jar.

4. Add star anise, cloves, citrus peels, and cover with 2 liters of vodka.

5. Seal tightly and shake.

6. Store at room temperature for 2 full weeks. Shake bottle every couple of days to expose the spices again.

7. Strain carefully through fine mesh, chinoise, or a gold coffee filter and rebottle.

8. Add 1 ounce demerara simple syrup (page 113) and shake well to incorporate.

9. Store in the freezer for best effect.

HORSERADISH VODKA
(NEW ENGLANDER)

1.75 liters bottle vodka

2 cups shredded peeled horseradish root

1. Place fresh horseradish in infusion container.

2. Top with full 1.75 liters of tequila.

3. Seal tightly and allow to infuse for 24–48 hours.

4. Strain and use with a splash of tomato juice in oyster shooter.

HORSERADISH TEQUILA
(EL CHULO)

1.75 liters bottle blanco tequila

2 cups shredded peeled horseradish root

1. Place fresh horseradish in infusion container.

2. Top with full 1.75 liters of tequila.

3. Seal tightly and allow to infuse for 24–48 hours.

4. Strain and use with a splash of tomato juice in an oyster shooter.

"I drink too much. The last time I gave a urine sample it had an olive in it."

— RODNEY DANGERFIELD

"I'm not quite sure where I stand on the legalization of drugs—though, if tequila is legal, pot should probably be legal."

—TED DEMME

LONDONER

1.75 liters gin

2 cups sliced English cucumber, peeled and seeded (half-moons)

Zest of 2 lemons

8 leafy sprigs of dill, bruised

1. Place cucumber, lemon zest, and dill in infusion jar.

2. Top with gin.

3. Allow to infuse 48–72 hours.

4. Strain and use with a small splash of lemon juice in oyster shooter

"Better belly burst than GOOD LIQUOR be lost."

— JONATHAN SWIFT

BANGKOK

1.75 liters vodka

½ cup peeled ginger, cut into small disks

2 stalks lemongrass, chopped

¾ cup fresh Thai basil leaves, bruised

1. Place ginger, lemongrass, and Thai basil leaves in infusion jar.

2. Top with vodka.

3. Allow to infuse 48–72 hours.

4. Strain and use with a small splash of lime juice in oyster shooter.

CHIHUAHUA

1.75 liters vodka

4 small Thai chili peppers, split and seeds removed (do with gloves)

8 sprigs of cilantro, bruised

1. Place peppers and cilantro in infusion jar.

2. Top with vodka. Allow to infuse 48–72 hours.

3. Strain and use with a splash of tomato juice in oyster shooter.

SERAFIN

1.75 liters vodka

4 serrano chili peppers, split and seeds removed, cut into rings (do with gloves)

12 sprigs of tarragon, bruised

1. Place peppers and tarragon in infusion jar.

2. Top with vodka.

3. Allow to infuse 48–72 hours.

4. Strain and use with a splash of pineapple juice in oyster shooter.

"The relationship between a Russian and a bottle of vodka is almost mystical."

— RICHARD OWEN

"PROHIBITION is better than no liquor at all."

— WILL ROGERS

FRANKLIN MORTGAGE & INVESTMENT CO.

(AL SOTACK)

Franklin Mortgage & Investment Co. is located in Philadelphia, Pennsylvania. The name pays tribute to the art and craftsmanship bartenders brought to the bar in the United States pre-Prohibition era. The name is borrowed from the late 1920s company that ran the biggest underground alcohol ring, even bigger than Al Capone's. They draw from their historical mentors, such as Jerry "The Professor" Thomas, Ada Coleman, and Harry Johnson.

All the following drinks by Al Sotack, former head bartender, Franklin Mortgage & Investment Co., Philadelphia, Pennsylvania.

RASPBERRY-INFUSED COGNAC

25 oz. cognac

½ cup or so raspberries

1. Muddle the raspberries and place in infusion jar.

2. Add cognac and cover for NO MORE THAN 24 HOURS. This infusion works best with tasting between 16 and 24 hours incrementally and pulling when done. You're looking to pull before a sort of "artificial" or metallic flavor sets in.

3. Strain. Sip.

WATERMELON AND CILANTRO INFUSED TEQUILA

25 oz. blanco tequila

Small watermelon

⅓ bushel cilantro

1. Cut about a dozen 2- to 3-inch cubes of watermelon and add to an infusion jar.

2. Add one-third bushel of cilantro.

3. Add the tequila.

4. Remove cilantro after 15–20 minutes and allow watermelon to sit for 5–7 hours.

5. Strain and serve.

JAMES BOND: "I never have more than one drink before dinner. But I do like that one to be large and very strong and very cold and very well made. This drink is my own invention. I'm going to patent it when I can think of a good name."

— IAN FLEMING, *CASINO ROYALE*

NATIONAL MECHANICS
(PAUL BROWN)

National Mechanics Bar and Restaurant is located in Old City, Philadelphia in a historic building built by William Strickland in 1837. Since then the building has housed banks, churches, and clubs. The bar's name originates from the building's first incarnation, the National Mechanics Bank. With a great mix of old-world feel and new-world charm, bartender Paul Brown entertains his guests with stellar infusions and remarkable cocktails in a laid-back atmosphere.

The following drinks are by Paul Brown, bartender, National Mechanics, Philadelphia, Pennsylvania.

APPLE WHISKEY

Our Apple Whiskey is made with Canadian Club Whiskey, cinnamon, cloves, vanilla extract, nutmeg, and whichever apples look good this week. For this, we do very little to make this into a Bonita Apple-bomb. Simply drop 1½ ounces of Apple Whiskey into ½ pint of Smithwick's Irish Ale and throw it back!

"I doubt if you can have a truly wild party without liquor."

— CARL SANDBURG

JALAPEÑO TEQUILA

Our jalapeño tequila is made starting with Siembra Azul Blanco Tequila. We add to it, cracked peppercorns and, of course, fresh jalapeños. From this we make a Pineapple Jalapeño Tequila Margarita, which is made with 1 ounce of homemade margarita mix, ½ ounce of pineapple juice, ½ ounce of Combier, and 1½ ounce of our Jalapeño Tequila.

"Drinking is a way of ending the day."

— ERNEST HEMINGWAY

BACON VODKA

Our Bacon Vodka is made with filtered vodka, thick bacon cooked lightly, and black pepper. Make sure some of the rendered fat is added to the vodka. We keep the fat in the infusion (it adds to the mystique of the libation), but if you want to take it out, strain it or put in the freezer to solidify the fat. Typically we just add this to Bloody Marys (delicious!) or for the bold, we make a Bacon Chocolate Martini.

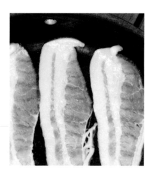  

Bacon Chocolate Martini

Mix 1 ounce Bacon Vodka with 1 ounce Godiva Chocolate Liqueur. Chill and serve into a martini glass rimmed with chocolate syrup.

Mixologist Q&A
PAUL BROWN

1. *How do you decide which flavors (essences) complement which liquors?* The flavors we've used typically come from consideration. Bacon Vodka was the first as a way to bacon-ize alcohol. Added to neutral vodka allows only the bacon flavoring to come through. Others we've dealt with have come up in conversation or just thinking that something may work. There have been failed experiments....

2. *When you create an infusion do you have a cocktail in mind to use it in?* When we make an infusion, we don't think too much about its use. It's alcohol, you can always find a use for it. Often, people (staff, patrons, anyone) will come up with a drink that (at least they think) is pretty good. I think the Bacon Vodka Jalapeño Tequila Martini was pretty horrific.

3. *What was the riskiest infusion you tried that ended up coming out great?* Before the iced tea vodkas became popular, I made a simple infusion of Lipton tea bags and cane sugar. At first, it was terrible; it had all of the bitterness and earthiness of tea with nothing else. Given more time, it had mellowed into a very tasty tincture.

4. Can you give home infusers any tips or advice? If anything I've learned to experiment without being too ambitious all at once. When first making an infusion, keep it simple. You don't want to spend a lot of time just to have it ruined by the third or fourth ingredient. Everything goes into a solution at different times, so there's no knowing what the contribution of several ingredients will be in a week or two.

5. How do you know when an infusion is perfect for serving or bottling? It's easy to know when it's ready because it tastes right. The challenge is sometimes you don't know if it's not ready yet or if it's already past its peak.

6. How long do most infusions take? It depends. For the infusions we use, they're ready in a week. Very bold flavors. If you're doing something subtle (like cucumbers or lemon zest) you'll need more time. It's all part of the fun. My favorite part is remembering something I have started but have forgotten—like this bourbon and cherries that has been sitting around for a year.

"I FEEL SORRY for people who don't drink. When they wake up in the morning, that's as good as they're going to feel all day."

— FRANK SINATRA

THE SMOKE JOINT
(JOHN HOFFER)

Owned by Ben Grossman and Craig Samuel, The Smoke Joint is located in Fort Greene, Brooklyn. Along with serving some of the best New York barbeque in a relaxed environment, manager John W. Hoffer offers his patrons some delicious cocktails created from house-made infusions.

The following drinks are by John Hoffer, manager of The Smoke Joint Restaurant Group, The Smoke Joint, Brooklyn, New York.

HABANERO & MANGO TEQUILA

Be careful, this infusion is spicy!

2 bottles of tequila (25 oz. each)

8 mangoes

1 habanero pepper

1. Peel and slice 8 mangoes and place into the bottom of the infusion jar.

2. Fill infusion jar with tequila.

3. Let infuse for 1 week.

4. Lightly fire roast 1 habanero pepper and place into infusion for 1 day.

5. Open infusion jar and discard the pepper.

6. Pour tequila through a strainer and mash the mango through the strainer into the tequila.

Here's a drink featuring Habanero & Mango Tequila.

Mango Margarita

1. Fill a tumbler with ice.
2. Pour in 2 ounces of Habanero & Mango Tequila and 1 ounce of Cointreau.
3. Fill the tumbler with limonade.
4. Shake, garnish with lime slice, salt the rim of the glass, and serve.

"NOTHING IS so musical as the sound of pouring bourbon for the first drink on a Sunday morning. Not Bach or Schubert or any of those masters."

— CARSON MCCULLERS, FROM
CLOCK WITHOUT HANDS

JALAPEÑO & LIME VODKA

This infused masterpiece is great for the sample cocktails that follow!

2 bottles of vodka (25 oz. each)

3 jalapeños

5 limes

1. Take 2 jalapeños and poke holes in them and place them into the bottom of an infusion jar.

2. Take the 1 remaining jalapeño and cut into ½-inch slices and place into infusion jar.

3. Take the 5 limes and cut the ends off and place each lime on end and cut in half, and cut into ½-inch slices and place limes into infusion jar.

4. Empty 2 bottles of vodka into jar.

5. Close infusion jar, date, and label.

6. Let sit for 1–2 weeks.

Here they are, the promised recipes featuring
Jalapeño & Lime Vodka.

Smoky Mary

1. Add cucumber slice, olive, four squirts of Holla (our house-made hot sauce) or other hot sauce, two squirts of Worcestershire sauce, a heaping bar spoon of horseradish, three shakes of celery salt, six shakes of pepper, and ½ ounce of lemon juice in a mixing glass.
2. Muddle contents and add 2 ounces of Jalapeño & Lime Vodka and 1 can of tomato juice. Shake.
3. Rim tumbler with 78 spice (our house-made rub for BBQ meats) or other BBQ spices.
4. Fill a glass with ice and pour shaken contents into the glass. Garnish with olive on a skewer and a lemon wedge on the rim of the glass.

Trouble Loves Me

1. Add 2 ounces of Jalapeño & Lime Vodka, 1 ounce of triple sec, 1¼ ounces limonade, and ¾ ounce of orange juice to a mixing glass.
2. Shake and strain into a chilled martini glass. Garnish with lime.

"We were not a hugging people. In terms of emotional comfort it was our belief that no amount of physical contact could match the healing powers of a well made cocktail."

— DAVID SEDARIS

SPICED PUMPKIN VODKA

2 bottles vodka
(25 oz. bottles)

Small sliced pumpkin

Cinnamon sugar

½ whole nutmeg

Cinnamon stick

3 cloves

1. Slice a small pumpkin into ½-inch slices and spread out on a sheet pan.

2. Dust the pumpkin slices with cinnamon sugar.

3. Place sheet pan in oven set at 350°F until pumpkin slices begin to brown. Set the sheet pan aside to cool.

4. Place the nutmeg, cinnamon stick, 3 cloves, the cooled off pumpkin slices, and the vodka into an infusion jar and seal.

5. Allow to infuse for 2 weeks.

6. After 2 weeks, strain the vodka, and then place only the pumpkin slices and vodka into blender and blend.

7. After being completely blended, strain the vodka through a strainer to get any large pieces out and now the infusion is ready to serve.

Here's a yummy cocktail featuring Spiced Pumpkin Vodka.

Roasted Pumpkin Spice Cocktail

1. Combine the following ingredients into a chilled cocktail glass: 3 ounces Spiced Pumpkin Vodka, 1½ ounces amaretto, and ½ ounce Baileys.
2. Garnish with toasted pumpkin seeds. (You can use seeds from the pumpkin you used to make the vodka infusion. Wash the seeds, spread them on a sheet pan, dust with cinnamon sugar, and toast them in the oven.)

"A man in Russia, who drank three bottles of vodka and survived a 50 foot fall from a balcony after he jumped to get away from his nagging wife, survived a second jump after his wife continued to nag him. I don't know what brand of vodka it was, but that should be the commercial for it."

—SETH MEYERS

STRAWBERRY & VANILLA BOURBON

2 bottles (25 oz.) bourbon

1 quart of rinsed and sliced strawberries

5 ounces sugar

Vanilla extract

2 whole vanilla beans

1. Hull strawberries and cut them in half.

2. Place strawberries in a bowl and put 5 ounces of vanilla-infused sugar on the top of the strawberries.

3. Place strawberries into the bottom of a clean infusion jar.

4. Cut a slit into both of the vanilla beans and place into the infusion jar.

5. Fill the infusion jar with 2 bottles (25 oz. bottles) of bourbon. Close lid.

6. Let infuse for 2 weeks.

Here are a few cocktails featuring Strawberry & Vanilla Bourbon.

Lafayette Limonade

1. Muddle a strawberry at the bottom of a tumbler. Fill with ice.
2. Pour 2 ounces of Strawberry & Vanilla Bourbon over the ice. Fill with limonade, shake, garnish with strawberry and lime, and serve.

Bourbon on Elliott

1. Combine the following ingredients in a tumbler: 1½ ounces Strawberry Vanilla Bourbon and 1 ounce Malibu.
2. Fill tumbler with orange juice, cranberry juice, and a splash of grenadine.
3. Fill rocks glass with ice.
4. Shake and pour back into glass. Garnish with a lime wedge.

"A drink a day keeps the shrink away."

— EDWARD ABBEY

JOHN W. HOFFER

1. How do you decide which flavors (essences) complement which liquors?
Vodkas are a little more giving as far as flavors to play with. So we have
a wide range of things to try and most end up working nicely. When you put
several ingredients into one infusion, you need flavors that complement each
other. So a little understanding of flavors and an imagination work well. For
bourbon, we choose flavors that already come through a bit in the bourbons,
such as cinnamon, vanilla, as well as cranberries and apples. For tequila,
mango and habanero just popped in my head immediately and it worked
beautifully. The fire-roasted habanero picks up on the light smokiness of
the tequila and the mango plays in perfectly with it.

2. When you create an infusion do you have a cocktail in mind to use it in?
I would say the majority of the time my mind starts working on a cocktail
after tasting the finished infusion and we work on it from there. Sure you
have ideas, but it may come out a little differently than expected.

3. *What was the riskiest infusion you tried that ended up coming out great?*
I would have to say the bacon bourbon. We used bacon, brown sugar, and black peppercorns. There is just something strange about bacon floating in a jar full of liquor. It's intriguing for customers to see. That is usually the first one they notice and ask about. Surprisingly everyone who tries it loves it. We are a wonderful BBQ restaurant, so a bacon bourbon fits right in—meat on your plate and smoked meat in your drink.

4. *Can you give home infusers any tips or advice?* Be experimental and you will be surprised by what pairings work. Also, infusions are great holiday and birthday gifts. For restaurants and bars they are a great backdrop for the bar and wonderful conversational pieces.

5. *How do you know when an infusion is perfect for serving or bottling?*
It's all about taste. I keep mine on a rotation of two weeks. Sure some can be used before then. But two weeks is what seems to work for the flavors I'm trying to reach and also for the rotation in our establishment.

6. *How long do most infusions last?* Our cocktail menu is based on our infusions, so we burn through them. All the alcohol we infuse with is 80 proof or higher, so the infusions can be kept a long time.

CIENFUEGOS
(JANE DANGER)

Cienfuegos is in the East Village in New York City. Located above the Cuban sandwich shop Carteles, Cienfuegos provides an all-encompassing experience into the port town of Cienfuegos, Cuba, serving all things rum. Mixologist Jane Danger concocts infused rums that are used in matchless cocktails and amazing punches.

The following drinks are by Jane Danger, Cienfuegos, New York City, New York.

RUM RAISIN

We use this in a Golden Fizz. We choose Mount Gay Gold because it tastes like a classic choice for imitating the flavor in rum-raisin ice cream. Infuse a liter of the Mount Gay Eclipse Gold and 2½ cups of raisins. Let this set for 24–48 hours. Strain and serve.

ROOIBOS TEA-INFUSED ELIJAH CRAIG 12-YEAR BOURBON

We use this in a punch with lemon and peach brandy. For this one I like how nutty both the tea and bourbon are. Infuse ¼ cup of loose tea leaves in 25 oz. of the bourbon. Let it set for 20 minutes, and then strain before drinking.

JANE DANGER

1. How do you decide which flavors (essences) complement which liquors?
I never try to change the overall flavor of a spirit. You want to choose
the base spirit that will best display your infusing ingredients.

2. When you create an infusion do you have a cocktail in mind to use it in?
Yes. Like for the Rum Raisin, I knew I wanted a dessert-style drink, like
a Flip or Golden Fizz.

3. What was the riskiest infusion you tried that ended up coming out great?
The riskiest infusion I did was probably my silliest—my Jelly Bean Gin, which I
did for my Jelly Bean Collins.

4. Can you give home infusers any tips or advice? When home infusing,
you should be very careful with teas, herbs, and coffee. Although the quickest
to make infusions with, they can become bitter and ruin your infusion very
easily. You must time them and taste as you go along to make sure you don't
overdo it.

5. How do you know when an infusion is perfect for serving or bottling?
I trust my own palate. Timing is always a good start for consistency.

6. How long do most infusions take? It depends on what you are infusing
and what spirit and strength you chose. Teas, herbs, and dried fruits are
very quick. Melons and berries are quick as well. Hard fruits take longer.
Chocolate and fatty things such as nuts and bacon need to be chilled and
then the fat has to be skimmed off after infusing.

KHONG RIVER HOUSE

*Located in Miami Beach, Florida, Khong River House
serves up delectable Southeast Asian fare as a tribute to
the Mekong region and offers an outstanding selection of spirits
and infusions. A crowd favorite is the "Porthole Infuser"—
a device capable of rapidly infusing herbs and botanicals.
Pick up one for yourself and create these libations at home
(www.theportholeinfuser.com). The following drinks are by 50
Eggs, Inc., Khong River House, Miami Beach, Florida.*

RAPID INFUSION NO. 1
THE GREY BERRY

Check out this unique blend of gin, brandy, and rum for a truly one-of-kind libation.

Infusion Ingredients:

Spring 44 Gin

Asbach Uralt Brandy

Appleton VX Jamaican Rum

Earl Grey tea

Fresh lemongrass

Allspice berries

Blackberries

Orange oil

Cocktail Ingredients:

Dry:

1 Allspice Berry (crushed or broken)

3 inches of lemongrass quartered lengthwise

2 tablespoons Earl Grey

6 blackberries (cut in half)

1 orange spiral (8- to 10-inch)

6 dashes orange bitters

Wet:

1¼ oz. Spring 44 Gin

1¼ oz. Asbach Uralt Brandy

1¼ oz. Appleton VX Jamaican Rum

2½ oz. White Ver Jus

1½ oz. simple syrup

1 oz. water

1. Crush allspice in a mixing tin.

2. Build all dry ingredients in the Porthole, add bitters, then seal and fill with pre-bottled infusion mix.

TIP

The Porthole is a simple, beautiful cold-infusion container designed by Martin Kastner of Crucial Detail design studio.

RAPID INFUSION NO. 2
THE KHONG RIVER HOUSE

Another gin, brandy, and rum infusion from Khong River House—but with a completely different flavor profile.

Infusion Ingredients:

Spring 44 Gin

Asbach Uralt Brandy

Appleton VX Jamaican Rum

Dried hibiscus flowers

Tahitian vanilla bean

Fresh galanga

Lemon peel

Served with a bottle of sparkling wine

Cocktail Ingredients:

Dry:

2 tablespoons hibiscus flowers

¼ vanilla bean (split)

6 galanga coins (¼-inch thick)

1 lemon spiral (8–10 inches)

6 dashes orange bitters

Wet:

1¼ oz. Spring 44 Gin

1¼ oz. Asbach Uralt Brandy

1¼ oz. Appleton VX Jamaican Rum

2½ oz. White Ver Jus

1½ oz. simple syrup (page 113)

1 oz. water

1. Bruise galanga in a mixing tin.

2. Build all dry ingredients in the Porthole, add bitters, then seal and fill with pre-bottled infusion mix.

TIP

Alpinia galanga—one of the ingredients in this infusion—is a member of the ginger family.

THE EVELEIGH

(DAVE KUPCHINSKY)

The Eveleigh lies on Sunset Boulivard in Los Angeles, California and has garnered a stellar reputation for both rustic farm-to-table fare and innovative libations. Head barman, Dave Kupchinsky, offers up unique cocktails made with in-house infusions and fresh garnishments. A true place to escape the bustle of LA while in LA.

The following drink is by Dave Kupchinsky, head barman, Eveleigh, Los Angeles, California.

EARL GREY INFUSED SHERRY

3 oz. of Earl Grey tea

1 bottle of
Amontillado sherry

1. Place tealeaves in bottom of infusion jar.

2. Add sherry and seal the jar.

3. Let sit for 3 hours.

4. Strain the sherry into a clean bottle and cap.

BERGAMOT SOUR

If you're a fan of bourbon and earl gray tea stop by the Eveleigh for this outstanding cocktail.

1 oz. Bonded Bourbon

1 oz. Earl Grey Sherry

½ oz. lemon juice

½ oz. Caribbean cane syrup

Mix together, shake and strain over ice and garnish with an orange twist.

RESOURCES & SUPPLIES

* For oak barrels, glycerin, and other supplies visit these sites:
http://www.eckraus.com/
http://www.1000oaksbarrel.com/

* If you want to try a new whiskey but don't feel like shelling out for a whole bottle, check out Drinks by the Dram, a company that offers samples of many fine whiskeys.
http://www.masterofmalt.com/drinks-by-the-dram/

* For whiskey information and supplies, visit Malt Advocate.
http://www.maltadvocate.com/

* Don't water down your whiskey. Use whiskey stones!
http://www.thinkgeek.com/caffeine/accessories/ba37/

* An online alcohol-by-volume calculator:
http://www.cleavebooks.co.uk/scol/ccalcoh4.htm

* Infusion jars:
http://www.infused-vodka.com/

* Check out these glass-infusion pitchers at Home-Decor.hsn.com:
http://home-decor.hsn.com/colin-cowie-flavor-infusing-glass-pitcher_p-5901466_xp.aspx

* For artificial flavorings for your cordials, check out these retailers:
http://www.shanks.com/
www.lorannoils.com/

* Create your very own ice spheres. Keep your whiskey cold but not watered down with the ice ball mold from Japantrendshop.com.
http://www.japantrendshop.com/ice-ball-mold-for-perfect-ice-spheres-p-244.html

* Have ice spheres delivered directly to your door (for a price) from glace-ice.com:
http://glace-ice.com/

* Create larger ice cubes with items such as a muffin pan available from many outlets including Amazon.com:
http://www.amazon.com/Kitchenaid-Wire-Sled-Muffin-Silicone/dp/B0000DC645/ref=pd_bbs_9?ie=UTF8&s=home-garden&qid=1214605815&sr=8-9

* Sit back and relax with *Whisky Magazine*.
http://www.whiskymag.com/

The American Distilling Institute is the creator of the annually published *Distiller's Resource Directory*, a book containing a compilation of distilling supply vendors and service providers. http://distilling.com

A great resource for the do-it-yourselfer! http://homedistiller.org

Go to school! http://www.artisancraftdistilling.com

Need distilling yeast? http://www.whitelabs.com

Although largely aimed at beer brewers, this website has many helpful articles for the home spirit distiller. http://www.probrewer.com

Get your still! https://www.moonshinestill.com

For distilling calculators, general information, purchasing grain (if you can't find a local supplier), and some inventive easy-to-use products, check out Hillbilly Stills. http://www.hillbillystills.com

A store and resource for many home distilling needs. http://www.home-distilling.com

Calculate your ABV (alcohol by volume)! http://www.brewersfriend.com

GLOSSARY

GLOSSARY

Alcohol by Volume (AbV): The standard measurement system used to determine the amount of alcohol contained within a total volume of liquid.

Blended Whiskey: Whiskey made from either two or more malt whiskeys or a mixture of grain and malt whiskeys.

Bourbon: Whiskey made in the United States containing, at minimum, 51 percent corn and stored for at least two years in new charred oak barrels. Many bourbon distilleries reside in Kentucky, but it is not a prerequisite for bourbon classification.

Cognac: French brandy.

Cordial: A term used in the Unites states for alcohol containing at least 2.5 percent sugar by weight. Many cordials contain much more than 2.5 percent.

Corn Whiskey: Whiskey that contains a minimum of 80 percent corn that is not required to be aged in wood.

Crème: An alcohol containing milk or cream that should be refrigerated.

Dram: An informal term for a small amount of whiskey.

Decanter: A vessel, often made of crystal, with a matching tight-fitting stopper used to hold liquids. Often used for holding wine or other liquor.

Infusion: The process of flavoring water and liquors with foods, herbs and spices, and other flavorings.

Maceration: An alternate term for infusion, more specifically relating to alcohol.

Malt: Grain that has been allowed to sprout.

Mash: A fermented malt or grain that is used to distill alcohol.

Liqueur: European equivalent term for cordial (used in the United States).

Neat: A bourbon/whiskey drink with nothing added (no ice). Also known as "straight."

Proof: The relative percentage of alcohol to water in a liquor. The origin of the proof measuring system, originally known as "gunpowder proof," came about as a method to "prove" or check the alcoholic content of liquor. Equal parts bourbon and gunpowder were mixed and lit on fire. If the result was a yellow flame, the alcohol was too strong and needed to be further diluted. When an alcohol's flame burned blue, it was known to be "true" and good to drink.

Rye Whiskey: Whiskey made from a minimum of 51 percent rye and matured in new charred oak barrels for at least two years. Rye whiskey must be distilled at less than 80 percent.

Scotch Whisky: Whisky made in Scotland matured for at least three years and one day in oak casks. Scotch is often (but not always) treated with peat smoke, giving its malt a unique smoky flavor.

Simple Syrup: Sweetening syrup made from equal parts sugar and water (see page 113).

Single Malt Whiskey: Whiskey made from one source of malted barley from one distillery.

Tennessee Whiskey: Whiskey made in Tennessee and filtered through sugar-maple charcoal.

Vatting/Vated: The process of blending whiskies at home.

Wheat Whiskey: Whiskey made from a minimum of 51 percent wheat. Wheat whiskey is the least common type.

Zest: The outer rind of citrus fruit comprised of the flavorful outer colored portion and the white bitter inner portion.

INDEX

ABOUT CIDER MILL PRESS
BOOK PUBLISHERS

Good ideas ripen with time. From seed to harvest, Cider Mill Press brings fine reading, information, and entertainment together between the covers of its creatively crafted books. Our Cider Mill bears fruit twice a year, publishing a new crop of titles each spring and fall.

Visit us on the Web at
www.cidermillpress.com
or write to us at
12 Spring Street
PO Box 454
Kennebunkport, Maine 04046